Other Titles in THE EERIE SERIES

GHOSTS
by Seymour Simon

MEET THE WEREWOLF
by Georgess McHargue

MOVIE MONSTERS
by Thomas G. Aylesworth

SPACE
MONSTERS

SPACE MONSTERS

From Movies, TV, and Books

SEYMOUR SIMON

J. B. Lippincott Company/Philadelphia and New York

The author would like to thank the following for providing the material indicated: Pages 9, 10, 28, 31, 32, 36, 37, 39, 42, 44, 60, 62, 66, 67: Photographs courtesy of The Museum of Modern Art, Film Stills Archive. Pages 15, 27, 30, 50, 54, 55, 57, 70, 72, 74, 77: Photographs courtesy of Movie Star News. Pages 15, 32: Photographs reprinted by permission of Twentieth Century-Fox. Pages 21, 22: Extracts from "Vault of the Beast" by A. E. van Vogt reprinted by permission of A. E. van Vogt. Page 31: Photograph copyright © 1958 by Paramount Pictures Corporation and William Alland Productions, Inc. Page 42: Photograph copyrighted, RKO General Pictures. All photographs not otherwise credited are from the author's personal archives.

The author would also like to extend his thanks to the following studios: Allied Artists, American International, Columbia, Mascot, MGM, Paramount, RKO, Twentieth Century-Fox, United Artists, Universal.

U.S. Library of Congress Cataloging in Publication Data

Simon, Seymour.
  Space monsters.

  (The Eerie series)
  Includes index.
  SUMMARY: Discusses some of the more prominent books, movies, and TV shows which have featured monsters and outer space settings.
    1. Monsters in mass media. 2. Science fiction—History and criticism. [1. Monsters. 2. Science fiction—History and criticism. I. Title.]
  P96.M6S5   791.43'7   77-3566
  ISBN-0-397-31765-4   ISBN-0-397-31766-2 (pbk.)

CONTENTS

For Robert and Michael

and the Monsters they love

1 · FIRST VISIT FROM MARS

The year is 1898. The place is a peaceful English village just outside London. It seems to be an unlikely place for a spaceship from the planet Mars to land. But this is the setting for the start of perhaps the most famous space monster story. The story's title is *The War of the Worlds*. Its author is H. G. Wells.

The story describes what happens when Martian invaders land on Earth. It is told by an English observer who lives in the village where the invasion begins. Here is how he describes his first view of a Martian:

But, looking, I presently saw something stirring within the shadow: grayish billowy movements, one above another, and then two luminous disks—like eyes. Then something resembling a little gray snake, about the thickness of a walking stick, coiled up out of the writhing middle and wriggled in the air toward me—and then another.

A big grayish rounded bulk, the size perhaps of a bear, was rising slowly and painfully out of the cylinder. As it bulged up and caught the light, it glistened like wet leather. Two large dark-colored eyes were regarding me steadfastly. The mass that framed them, the head of the thing, it was rounded, and had, one might say, a face. There was a mouth under the eyes, the lipless brim of which quivered and panted, and dropped saliva. The whole creature heaved and pulsated convulsively.

When the first meeting between humans and Martians takes place, the invaders say nothing. They greet a flag of truce with a heat ray that destroys the humans. Soon they are on the march to London. Nothing that the human defenders do seems to be able to prevent the Martians from destroying all of humanity. They have intelligences greater than ours, just as ours are greater than those of animals. The Martians want the planet Earth for themselves.

An invading Martian from *War of the Worlds* (Paramount).

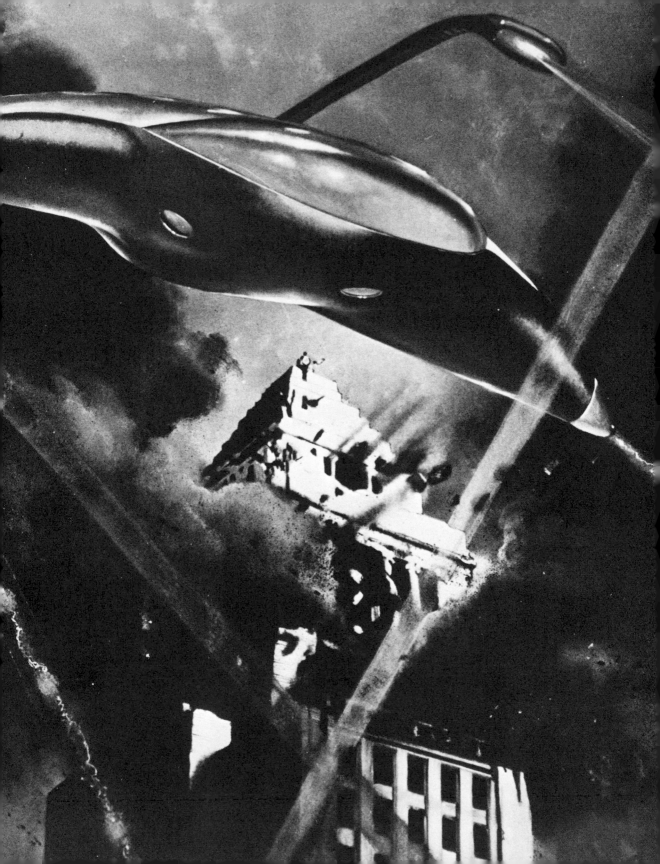

Without mercy, they set out to kill all the humans who live here.

Wells was not just trying to scare his readers. His story is the first description of what the horrors of modern war would be like. In the story he wonders if humans would really act so differently from the Martian invaders. "And before we judge them too harshly, we must remember what ruthless and utter destruction our own species [humankind] has wrought, not only upon animals, but upon its own races."

In the end, the invasion from Mars fails. But the invaders are not defeated by anything human. Our guns and fighting ability are useless against the Martians' superior knowledge and science. The Martians are finally destroyed by some of the lowest forms of life on earth—ordinary germs. The germs are harmless to humans who have become accustomed to them. But they are new and deadly to the Martians.

Wells is the author of many other books that have become classics of science fiction. Among the best-known are *The Time Machine, The Invisible Man, The*

Martian spaceships on the attack in *War of the Worlds*.

Island of Dr. Moreau, and *The Shape of Things to Come.* In his stories, Wells often comes up with great science fiction ideas.

For example, here is a passage from the first paragraph of *The War of the Worlds.* It could easily be the beginning of almost every space invasion story ever written.

Across the gulf of space, minds that are to our minds as ours are to those of the beasts that perish, intellects vast and cool and unsympathetic, regarded this earth with envious eyes, and slowly and surely drew their plans against us.

2·GREEN MEN OF MARS

Monsters from Mars figure in another early science fiction story. Only this time it is a human who travels to Mars. The story first appeared in 1912 as a six-part serial in a magazine. Its title was *Under the Moons of Mars.* It was later retitled *A Princess of Mars.* The author, Edgar Rice Burroughs, also wrote *Tarzan of the Apes.*

A Princess of Mars begins with the hero, John Carter, fleeing from pursuing Indians in Arizona. He hides in a cave and falls into a strange sleep. He hears some odd moans behind him in the darkness. His spirit is freed from his body and goes outside the cave.

Carter's spirit looks up at the night sky. A bright red star draws his attention. It is the planet Mars. Carter closes his eyes and stretches out his arms toward Mars. In some mysterious way, he is drawn through the cold and darkness of space to the distant red planet.

Carter awakens on Mars in a most peculiar position: he is hatching from an egg in a great incubator filled with eggs. He is immediately attacked by Tars Tarkas, a Green Martian who is fifteen feet tall. It's only because the gravity of Mars is less than he's accustomed to that John Carter can leap aside and save his life.

The planet Mars, or Barsoom, as Burroughs called it, is a strange and wonderful place. Barsoom is a dying world of red deserts. Its small seas are drying up. Its thin air has to be manufactured in a giant atmosphere factory. Many old civilizations once flourished on Barsoom. But their cities are deserted and little is left of their mighty buildings but ruins.

Yet Mars is still inhabited by many different races of creatures. The human-looking Red Men are the most civilized. They have rifles and airships driven by the mysterious "Eighth Ray." They run the air factory. But even the Red Men are warlike. Strangely, they prefer to fight with swords rather than with their guns.

Carter falls in love with a princess, Deja Thoris, a beautiful Red Woman. All Martian women lay eggs which hatch in incubators. In some unexplained way

Another Martian, this one in a baggy green skin, appears in *Invaders from Mars* (20th Century-Fox).

Carter and Deja Thoris have a son who hatches from an egg.

The Green Martians are primitive and even more warlike than the Red Martians. The Green Martians are twice as tall as humans, have four arms, gleaming white tusks, and eyes mounted on stalks. They hunt in bands along the dead ocean floors, riding ten-foot-tall, eight-legged mounts. The Green Men live in the magnificent ruined cities that dot the edges of the dead seas.

In later adventures, Carter meets Yellow Men hunting wild apelike creatures. The great white apes of Barsoom are fifteen feet tall and, like the Green Men, have four arms. Their noses and teeth are like those of African gorillas. And, like all the creatures of Barsoom, they are tough in a fight.

Carter also discovers Black Men, who are pirates, a race of headless humans, a race of cannibals, weird plants and animals, many strange ruins, and much more. Carter has one adventure after another, and becomes the greatest fighting man on Mars.

John Carter's story was so popular that Burroughs followed up *A Princess of Mars* with ten more books about Mars. The last of these, *John Carter of Mars,* was published in 1964, after Burroughs' death.

In addition to the Mars books, Burroughs wrote

two dozen Tarzan books; a series of books about a strange world named Pellucidar within a hollow Earth; *The Moon Maid,* about an inner world on the moon; and *The Land That Time Forgot,* about a lost world on Earth.

Burroughs also wrote four books about an Earth hero who goes to the planet Venus. Burroughs' Venus always keeps the same face turned to the sun. It has a hot tropical region with mile-high trees growing up into a wet atmosphere. It also has regions of ice and snow. Despite the exotic setting, the Venus books somehow don't have quite the same zip as the ones about Mars.

Burroughs wrote so many books that he finally founded his own publishing company in Tarzana, California. During his lifetime, his fifty-nine titles sold many millions of copies all over the world. Even today, they are still being bought and read by those who enjoy a good adventure story set in distant places of the imagination.

3·THE RISE OF THE BEMs

During the 1930s and the 1940s, science fiction stories became more and more popular. Many magazines devoted just to science fiction appeared on the newsstands. The magazines were called "pulps" because they were printed on a cheap, rough paper made from wood pulp.

The science fiction pulps competed with one another and with other kinds of pulp magazines for readers. The covers of the magazines were very important in this competition. The idea was to make the cover so interesting that the magazine would be picked out and bought.

Science fiction pulps usually tried to make their covers exciting by showing a space monster. The monster was often shown in the act of carrying away some pretty girl in a space suit. Other covers showed a monster attacking a city, a spaceship, or a group of

humans. The space monsters in these cover drawings were called BEMs by the readers of the magazines. BEM stood for Bug-Eyed Monster.

Some of the science fiction magazines of those years were *Amazing Stories, Fantastic Stories, Wonder Stories, Startling Stories,* and *Astounding Stories.* These are only a few of the many, many science fiction magazines which have been published. Some of the magazines lasted for many years, others for only one or two issues.

The stories inside the magazines were even more exciting than the covers. In 1928, E. E. Smith began to write stories about human heroes traveling all over the galaxy to battle evil forces that wanted to

take over space. These "space operas" were very popular. They featured all kinds of great inventions: needle rays, space axes, tractor beams, Q-guns, thought screens, spaceships that could travel faster than the speed of light, and much more. And the bad guys in the stories were really bad—and horrible to look at as well.

Smith's stories have titles such as "Skylark of Space," "Galactic Patrol," "Grey Lensman," and "Children of the Lens." They give a picture of a galaxy filled with inhabited planets where men in spaceships can roam among the stars and have fantastic adventures.

Another science fiction writer who created some great monsters was A. E. van Vogt. In stories such as "Vault of the Beast," "Not Only Dead Men," "Black Destroyer," and "Discord in Scarlet," van Vogt wrote about terrifying creatures that seem to come out of a nightmare. Here is an example from "Vault of the Beast":

> The creature crept. It whimpered from fear and pain. Shapeless, formless thing yet changing shape and form with each jerky movement, it crept along the corridor of the space freighter.

Later in the story:

> The floor moved under him, a visible wave that reared brown and horrible before his . . . eyes and grew into . . . a hissing mass. A venomous demon head reared on twisted, half-human shoulders . . . hands on apelike, malformed arms clawed at his face.

There are many science fiction writers who turned out exciting stories for the pulps. Robert Heinlein, Isaac Asimov, John Campbell, Henry Kuttner, L. Sprague de Camp, Theodore Sturgeon, Jack Williamson, and Frederic Pohl are just some of the science fiction greats from that period. Many of the stories first printed in the pulps are still available in paperback books.

Some of the best stories from the pulps contain very strange kinds of space monsters. For example, in one story by Sturgeon called "Killdozer!," an alien mind takes over a bulldozer and operates its controls. The machine tries to kill a construction worker who fights against it with the use of other machines.

A story called "The Cloak of Aesir" by Campbell

Arthur C. Clarke, author of *2001: A Space Odyssey*, has come a long way from his early days writing for the pulps.

is a weird mixture of science and supernatural powers. Campbell writes of the strange rulers of a defeated earth. Aesir is telepathic. He reads minds and speaks mind to mind. He is able to kill by touch. Yet the story also talks about an atomic blast capable of destroying half a cubic mile of matter.

Other monsters from outer space that appeared in pulp magazines include killer robots, giant reptiles, mind-reading aliens, insectlike races, and space beings that float between planets. The funny thing about them is that most of the monsters have eyes that bulge or stick out. They really are BEMs.

BEMs are still popular. Here are two from the movie *Invasion of the Saucer Men* (American International).

4 · ROBOTS GOOD AND EVIL

The word *robot* comes from a play titled *R.U.R.*, written by Karl Capek. The initials stand for Rossum's Universal Robots. In the play, the robots are flesh-and-blood creatures. But since the play's first performance in 1921 the word *robot* has come to mean "mechanical men."

Many robot stories have been written since *R.U.R.* Among the most interesting are those by Isaac Asimov. Asimov wrote a whole series of robot stories that were first published in science fiction pulp magazines. Later the stories were collected into two books, *I Robot* (1950) and *The Rest of the Robots* (1964).

Asimov's robots look just the way you would imagine: they have humanlike shapes with mechanical features. His robots are built to serve people in many ways. The robots are stronger than humans, last longer, can act quickly, and can even think more rapidly under certain conditions. They are also very likable, nicer than most of the humans in Asimov's stories.

Built into each robot are Asimov's Three Laws of Robotics:

1. A robot may not injure a human being or, through inaction, allow a human being to come to harm.

2. A robot must obey the orders given to it by a human being except where such orders would conflict with the First Law.

3. A robot must protect its own existence as long as such protection does not conflict with the First or Second Law.

The Three Laws seem to rule out any chance that a robot could do something wrong. Yet that's exactly what happens in Asimov's stories. It becomes the task of Dr. Susan Calvin, a robot psychologist, to find out why. Most often the fault lies not with the robots but with the humans in the story.

There have been many other likable robots in science fiction. Clifford D. Simak, in a series of stories collected in the book *City* (1952), writes of the sad robots left behind on Earth. Most of the humans have been destroyed in an atomic war. The survivors

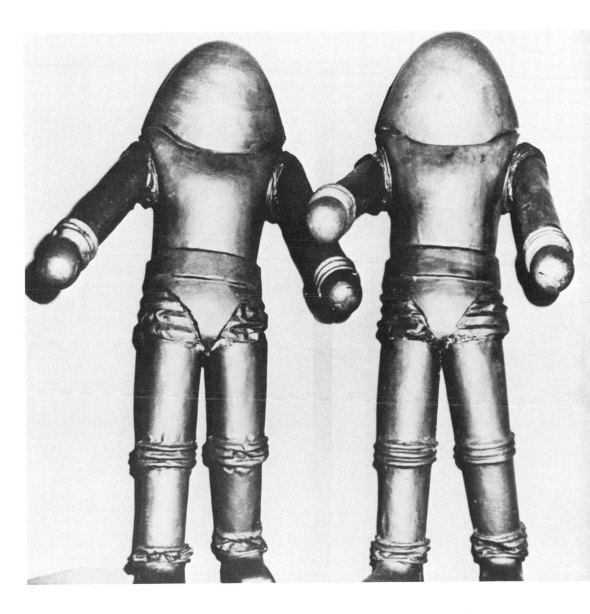

Many movies had mechanical-looking robots. These are from
Earth vs. the Flying Saucers (Columbia).

have emigrated to Jupiter. Only a few humans and a race of intelligent dogs remain on Earth.

The stories are about what happens when the robots have no one to serve and little work left to do. The robots make you feel sad and sorry for them.

But not all science fiction robots are so likable. Some are monsters. In a movie about a mechanical

A more human-looking robot is an advance scout for an invasion in *The Man from Planet X* (United Artists).

monster from space, called *Kronos* (1957), the robot is hundreds of feet tall. Kronos comes to Earth by way of a flying saucer. Its mission is to collect and store all of Earth's electric and atomic power. Kronos destroys buildings and power plants, kills people, and generally behaves like an unwelcome guest. Jet planes and an atomic bomb have little effect on Kronos. Finally all of Earth's stored power is turned against the huge robot, and at last Kronos is destroyed.

Another giant robot from space is seen in the Japanese film *The Mysterians* (1958). As usual with these giant robots, several cities are leveled and many people are killed before the robot is destroyed.

Sometimes robots become monsters because they are under an evil influence. In the movie *Gog* (1954), two robots called Gog and Magog are built to do simple tasks in an underground laboratory. The humans in the lab are working to develop a space station. But rays from a mysterious aircraft make the robots turn on their human masters. Finally Gog and Magog are destroyed along with the strange airship.

Other kinds of monster robots include the one in the film *Colossus of New York* (1958). The twelve-foot robot in the film looks something like a statue. It has a man's brain, but it behaves most unpleasantly to-

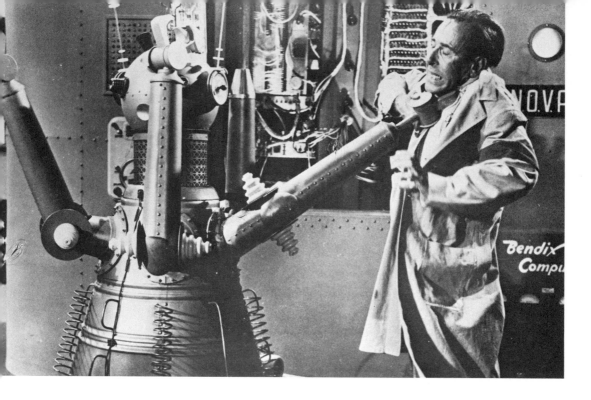

A robot turns against its maker in *Gog* (United Artists).

ward people. In a film called *Target Earth* (1954), the human hero wakes up to find his city deserted. The city was invaded by robots from outer space, and the humans left.

Perhaps the most familiar of all movie robots is Robby in *Forbidden Planet* (1956). (For the story of the film and a picture of Robby, see pages 61–62.) Robby the Robot is about the fanciest robot you will ever see in films. Most of the wind-up robots that are sold as toys seem to be patterned after Robby. The televi-

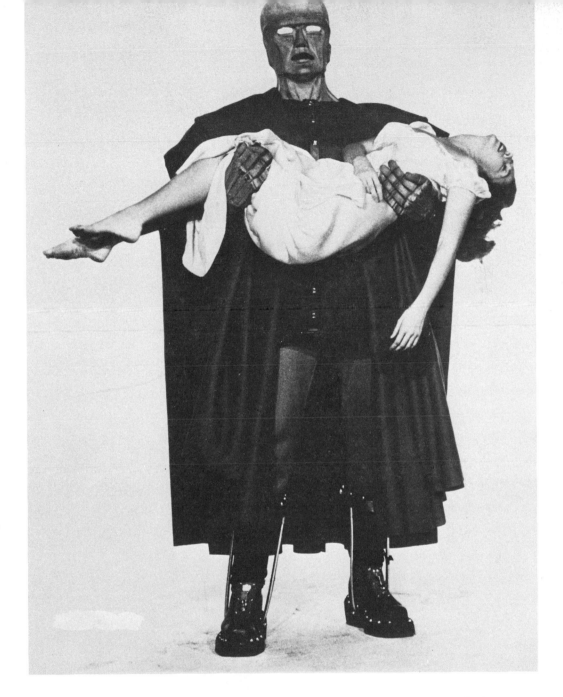

Carrying a girl is easy if you're a twelve-foot robot like the Colossus of New York (Paramount).

sion series "Lost in Space" also had a robot that looked much like Robby.

The most thought-provoking of the movies that have robot characters is probably *The Day the Earth Stood Still* (1951). In the film, a human-looking visitor from space named Klaatu comes to Earth accompanied by a ten-foot robot named Gort. Klaatu and Gort have come to Earth to warn humans that if they continue to misuse atomic weapons they will destroy

Patricia Neal is a temporary captive of Gort, the robot from *The Day the Earth Stood Still* (20th Century-Fox).

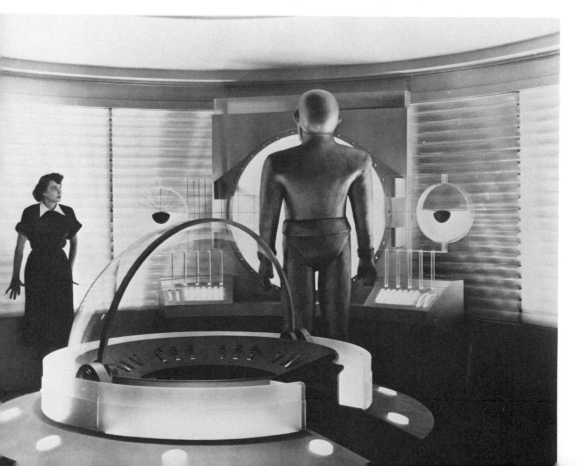

themselves and their planet as well. To show the power that he has at his disposal, Klaatu shuts down all of Earth's electrical energy for a half hour.

But Klaatu is shot to death by a human. His corpse is recovered by an angry Gort. Klaatu is brought back to life inside the flying saucer. Before returning to his distant home in space, Klaatu delivers this warning:

"Soon one of your nations will apply atomic power to rockets. Up to now we have not cared how you solved your petty squabbles. But if you threaten to extend your violence, this Earth of yours will be reduced to a burned-out cinder. Your choice is simple. Join us and live in peace. Or pursue your present course and face obliteration. The decision rests with you."

The film's plot was taken largely from a magazine story by Harry Bates called "Farewell to the Master." Klaatu gets killed in the story too. Humans go to the robot Gort and urge him to take back their apologies to his masters on the planet from which he came. "You don't understand," Gort replies. "I am the master."

5·MONSTERS FROM THE SERIALS

One of the first comic strip heroes in science fiction was Buck Rogers. Buck was a clean-cut, athletic, adventurous, twentieth-century youth. Trapped by radioactive gas in an abandoned mine, Buck loses consciousness. This happens in 1918. When he awakens he is in the twenty-fifth century.

Soon Buck is up to his neck in thrilling adventures. He rescues a young woman from danger. This gets to be a habit, for she becomes his sweetheart and he saves her dozens of times thereafter. In the world of the twenty-fifth century, Mongols have overrun America and Killer Kane, their leader, is out to conquer the world. Buck must fight against the evil plans of the villains.

Buck's adventures include landings on the moon, battles against an invasion from Mars, and an expedition to the lost continent of Atlantis. He fights against evildoers with all kinds of futuristic gadgets such as rockets, blasters, and fantastic machines. For a long time, the name Buck Rogers meant science fiction to youngsters.

The next important science fiction hero of the comic strips was Flash Gordon. Flash, his sweetheart Dale, and Professor Zarkov fought against the arch-villain Emperor Ming, ruler of the planet Mongo.

In 1936, a movie serial was made from the comic strip. Each week, another chapter of the serial would play at local film houses. The chapters always ended with what looked like certain death or destruction for Flash or his friends. But, sure enough, the next chapter saw them rescued in the nick of time.

There were two more movie serials in later years featuring Flash Gordon. While the plots were very much alike, the monsters were very different. Lion-men, Treemen, Hawkmen, Tigrons, Sharkmen, moving masses of living clay, Rockmen, and many other monsters were overcome by Flash Gordon week after week.

Buster Crabbe was the actor who played Flash Gordon. In 1939, he returned in the title role of a Buck Rogers film serial. The serial follows the original comic strip in having the hero put to sleep for five hundred years by Nirvano gas. He is awakened

Buck Rogers is menaced
by the evil Zuggman
(Universal).

just in time to fight against the evil plots of Killer
Kane and the Zuggs of Saturn.

There were many other science fiction movie serials.
Most of them featured monsters from outer space,
or evil robots, or a lost civilization from beneath
Earth's crust or the sea.

Even cowboys got into the act. In *Phantom Empire*
(1935), Gene Autry finds an entrance to Murania on
his cattle ranch. Murania is a scientific civilization
that exists thousands of feet below the surface of
Earth. It is ruled by Queen Tika and menaced by the

traitor Lord Argo. Autry is actually killed by the evil-doers, but Queen Tika is able to bring him back to life.

Undersea Kingdom (1936) features the lost continent of Atlantis. Atlantis has long ago sunk beneath the waves, but the Atlanteans are now preparing to invade the world on the surface. A scientific expedi-

An ad for the serial *Flash Gordon* (Universal).

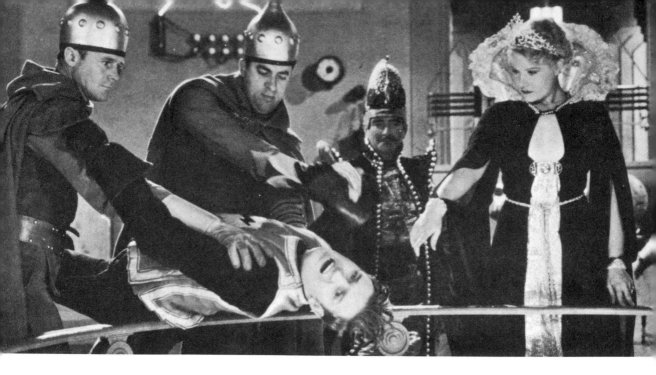

Gene Autry is a prisoner in *The Phantom Empire* (Mascot).

tion from aboveground arrives just in time. The humans fight against robots known as Volkites, who use ray guns. As usual, by the end of the serial the heroes have defeated the evil Unga Khan, leader of the Atlanteans.

In *The Phantom Creeps* (1939), Bela Lugosi, well-known for his role as the vampire in *Dracula,* plays the evil scientist Dr. Alex Zorka. Dr. Zorka finds a meteor that gives him the power to put people to sleep. Zorka sets out to conquer the world with the aid of a large robot and a belt of invisibility. Luckily

38

for the world, the good Dr. Mallory is able to defeat the evildoers.

The Mysterious Dr. Satan (1940) also has a mad doctor, along with another giant robot, out to conquer the world. This time, the world is saved by Copperhead, a good guy who wears a hood.

The world is in danger from still another source in *Flying Disc Man from Mars* (1951). The evil Mota lands his flying saucer in a volcano, which turns out to be not such a good idea. At the end of a dozen

Dr. Zorka and the evil robot from *The Phantom Creeps* (Universal).

chapters, the volcano explodes and ends his evil plans.

While all this is happening on Earth, evildoings are afoot deep in space. The bad Dr. Grood is seen at work in the 1953 serial *The Lost Planet*. Grood has enslaved Earthlings to work in the mines on the planet Ergro. The mines yield a metal called cosmonium. As we all know, when cosmonium is mixed with dornite it gives off a deadly ray. But once again Earth is saved by the good guys.

Meanwhile, back on Earth, moonmen are invading in *Radar Men from the Moon* (1952). Not to be outdone, an invader from Mercury menaces Earth in *Commando Cody* (1953). Still another invader from Mercury, this time the beautiful lady Rula, journeys to the *Mysterious Island* (1951) in search of a metal to destroy Earth.

These science fiction movie serials were just for fun. They had monsters, thrilling escapes, good-looking heroes and heroines, and mad scientists out to conquer the world. They probably had more fights and thrills per minute than any other action movies ever made. Some TV stations are still broadcasting some of the old serials like *Flash Gordon*. If you ever get a chance to see one, tune in and enjoy yourself.

6 · PLANT MONSTERS FROM SPACE

You never see the monster very clearly in *The Thing from Another World* (1951). Most of the filming is done in shadows. Your imagination makes the monster seem even more frightening. The monster is actually a plantlike being which needs blood to survive. The giant vegetable is played by James Arness, better known for his later TV work as Marshal Matt Dillon.

The Thing begins when a far northern U.S. military base receives a message about a UFO crashing near a scientific expedition to the North Pole. Sent to investigate, a plane crew arrives just before a blizzard.

The men walk out to the area of the crash. They look below the ice and see the outlines of some strange craft. Spacing themselves around the craft, they form a circle. As they look at one another they

These harmless-looking plants are really seedlings of the Thing (RKO). Their plant food is blood plasma.

realize that a flying saucer is trapped below the ice.

Unfortunately, a thermite bomb set off to melt the ice sets fire to the alien ship. It is completely destroyed. But the men are able to save the body of a crew member. The body is frozen solid in a large block of ice.

Back at the base, the block of ice is placed in a

storage room. The windows of the room are smashed so that the cold will prevent the ice from melting. But the block is accidentally covered by an electric blanket. Drip by drip, the ice melts, eventually releasing the creature, which escapes out the window.

One of the most frightening scenes takes place in a dark, crowded room at the camp. The soldiers are waiting in ambush. A beeping Geiger counter warns of the approach of the Thing. The beeps grow more rapid. Suddenly the door is flung open and the monster bursts into the room. It is quickly doused with kerosene and set afire. There is a suspenseful battle. Then the flaming Thing leaps through the window into the Arctic blackness.

The Thing is not yet finished. The final battle takes place in a darkened hallway. The Thing is finally destroyed by electricity. As the monster shrinks under the electric sparks, it gives off an odor like that of cooked cabbage.

One of the best movies about an invasion from space doesn't even have a scary-looking monster in it. Unless, of course, you count giant seedpods as scary-looking. The movie is called *Invasion of the Body Snatchers* (1956). The title is the least interesting part of the movie.

The story takes place in a small town in California. At the start, a young boy is running down a road. He is stopped by a car which the hero, played by Kevin McCarthy, is driving. The young boy is running away, he explains, because his mother isn't his mother anymore.

In the days that follow, McCarthy begins a romance with Dana Wynter. They hear many more strange stories of people who have changed in odd ways. Finally McCarthy is shown a half-formed body

Kevin McCarthy is shown his friend's double in *Invasion of the Body Snatchers* (Allied Artists).

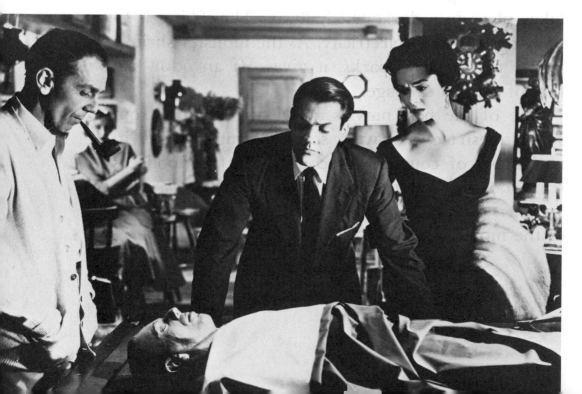

which was discovered in a friend's cellar. The body is a perfect duplicate of his friend.

Later McCarthy and his friend discover a greenhouse full of ripening pods. Each pod explodes and forms into a blank figure of a human being. The two humans destroy the blanks with pitchforks.

But it is soon too late to do anything. McCarthy and Dana Wynter are the last real humans left in the town. The pods have taken over everybody else. Out of a window the two watch the invasion taking place. A fleet of trucks pulls into the town square. Pods are unloaded from the trucks and carried off in all directions.

The human couple escape into the desert. They are tired but do not dare to sleep. Finally they hide in a deserted tunnel. McCarthy hears a noise and goes to find out what's happening. When he gets back, he finds Wynter asleep. He kisses her and she awakens. But as her eyes open, you realize that she too has become a pod person.

McCarthy runs away in desperation. On a nearby highway, he tries to flag down cars and trucks. "You're next," he yells as the cars whiz by. But nobody will stop. In the final scenes, one of the trucks carrying pods is in an accident. With the pods as evidence, McCarthy is able to convince some humans that an invasion is taking place. As the movie ends, there is hope that Earth will be saved.

The Day of the Triffids (1962) features still another invasion by plants. This time the plants arrive on Earth during a meteor shower. The people on Earth who have witnessed the brilliant display of meteors are all blinded. Only a small handful who did not view the shower are still able to see.

One of the most disturbing scenes takes place in an airliner. The pilot, crew, and all the passengers are blinded. No one can help them, and the plane crashes.

The plants in *The Day of the Triffids* (Allied Artists) are murderous invaders from space.

Soon the ten-foot triffids are on the march. Their deadly stinger vines claim victim after victim. At first the triffids are fought by fire. But it does not hold them back. Then the best weapon to use against the triffids is found by accident. A lighthouse keeper, who still has his sight because he was too drunk to watch the meteors, sprays seawater on the triffids. The seawater destroys the monster plants. And Earth is saved again.

7·INVADERS FROM SPACE

There have been so many stories and movies about invasions from space that if they were real there would be no room for all of the invaders to be on Earth. From H. G. Wells' tentacled Martians in *The War of the Worlds* to the comic invader played by Jerry Lewis in *Visit to a Small Planet* (1960), Earth seems to have been visited by just about everybody (and everything) in outer space.

One of the better movies about an invader is *It Came from Outer Space* (1953). The movie is frightening because it allows our imaginations to work instead of showing us a fake-looking monster made out of plaster and paint.

The movie begins in a small town in the Arizona desert. It is early evening. A young astronomer, played by Richard Carlson, sees a spaceship land and bury itself somewhere out in the desert. He tries to tell the townspeople but no one believes him.

A week goes by but Carlson can't find the ship. Suddenly two electric linemen disappear while working out in the desert. When they reappear they seem different in odd ways. One of them stares up at the blazing sun without blinking.

Soon other people begin to change. Carlson's girlfriend faces him on a windy hillside at night. He shivers in the chill and draws his clothing tightly together, but she stands untroubled by the cold wind.

Carlson finally is able to convince the people in the town that something strange is going on. But the alien visitors meet with Carlson. They tell him that something has happened to their spaceship and that they are just stopping on Earth to repair it. As soon as the ship is fixed, they say, they will leave. All the humans will be returned to normal. Carlson decides to give the aliens time to escape, and he seals the mine in which they are hiding. The invaders keep their promise; they release the humans and then they leave.

I Married a Monster from Outer Space (1958) sounds like a joke rather than a movie. Surprisingly, it is an interesting story that is well told. A young man who is to get married the next day is coming home at night from a party. He witnesses the landing of a

spaceship. Aliens appear and one of them takes over his shape. He is to be an advance scout for an invasion.

The next morning the alien in human shape is married. The mistakes he makes at the wedding are thought to be caused by a hangover from the party the previous night. The night after the wedding the alien is standing on a balcony during a thunderstorm. He is startled by a sudden flash of lightning. In the bright flash his human face dissolves into that of a hideous monster.

The monster was played by the actor Tom Tryon. He must have liked something about his role. Years later Tryon wrote a best-selling book about the supernatural called *The Other*.

An even more peculiar monster threatens Earth in *The Monolith Monsters* (1957). Again the setting is a small desert town. A meteorite carrying an alien substance crashes to Earth. The substance expands when it comes in contact with water. Only salt can prevent the substance from expanding.

Humans touched by the alien substance are

A good picture of the bridegroom from *I Married a Monster from Outer Space* (Paramount).

turned to giant, spearlike stones, or monoliths. The stone advances everywhere. The monoliths fall and shatter, only to spring up again. Frightening scenes include one in which a man turned to stone falls to the floor with a thundering crash, and one that shows a child whose lungs and arms are slowly being turned to stone.

Three science fiction films were made about a character from British TV named Dr. Bernard Quatermass. Two of the films are quite good. The first of the films was called *The Quatermass Experiment* (1955). In a later release it was titled *The Creeping Unknown*. In the film, a spaceship returns to Earth with only a single survivor. He is not in such good shape. He seems to be slowly turning into a large-sized plant that looks like a giant cactus. The film follows his wanderings through the slums and backways of London.

The last Quatermass film is the best. In Britain it was called *Quatermass in the Pit*. Its American title is *Five Million Years to Earth* (1968). Workers in London uncover a buried spaceship. Inside the ship they discover the decayed remains of alien creatures. The creatures have been buried in the ship since prehistoric times.

The ship also contains the skulls of Earthmen,

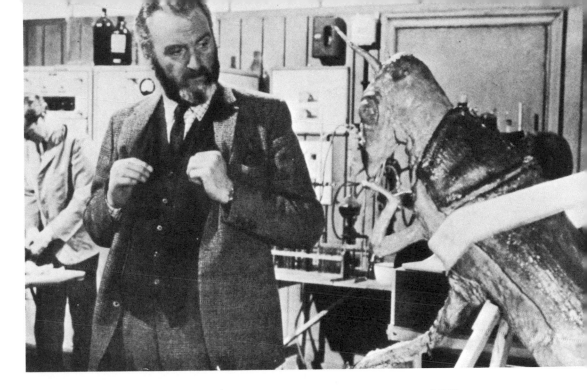

The ages-old remains of a space monster from *Five Million Years to Earth* (20th Century-Fox/Hammer).

changed to increase their brain size and intelligence, and ancient drawings of demons and monsters. It seems that the aliens had tried to take over Earth but had failed.

Although the aliens (which look like giant metallic grasshoppers) are dead, their ship is still in working order. By drawing on the mental power of Londoners, the ship tries to take over the city. The ship is finally destroyed when a giant steel crane is thrust through its body.

One of the more interesting giant monsters from outer space came to visit us in the film *Twenty Million Miles to Earth* (1957). The monster is brought back as an egg by the first expedition to Venus. The egg hatches and the monster starts to grow . . . and grow . . . and grow.

The Ymir takes a walk through Rome in *Twenty Million Miles to Earth* (Columbia).

The full-grown monster, known as Ymir, is a twenty-five-foot-tall reptile. It rampages through the ruins of Rome, destroying whatever it finds. One scene takes place in the Roman Colosseum, where animals and gladiators battled over two thousand years ago. This time the battle is between Ymir and

Battle of the heavyweights: the Ymir vs. an elephant in the Colosseum.

an elephant. A filming process called Dynamation was used to make the battle look almost real.

On and on came the monster invasion from outer space. In *The Crawling Eye* (1958), the space monsters make a cloud to cover their hideout in the Alps. After killing several mountain climbers, the monsters begin to move. Their target is a small town at the base of the mountain. The title of the movie tells you what to expect the monsters to look like.

The Blob (1958) featured another space monster which landed in the same year as the Eye. This gooey mass from space engulfed whatever was in its path, including people. A young Steve McQueen stars in the movie. The Blob is finally subdued by being frozen and dropped to the ice fields of the Arctic. But the Blob must be doing something up there. *Son of the Blob* was the 1972 sequel to the original messy eater.

In *Invaders from Mars* (1953), a small boy wakes up in the middle of the night and sees the arrival of a flying saucer. After that, things begin to change. The boy becomes aware that some grown-ups, including his father, aren't the same anymore.

Terror mounts as more and more adults are changed. Finally the boy is able to convince a few people that something's happening. The Martian

Even the Blob had to start out small (Paramount).

base is attacked. The Martians are green and woolly. (A picture of one is on page 15.) Their leader is a head in a transparent globe. In the end, it all turns out to be a bad dream . . . but not too bad a movie.

In *It Conquered the World* (1956), batlike creatures sweep down on humans and implant tiny radios in their necks. The bats are messengers for an evil visitor from Venus. One memorable scene from the movie takes place when a possessed wife greets her homecoming husband with the line, "A present for you, darling." Smiling, she throws a bat at him.

Monsters from outer space can sometimes be no larger than germs. In fact, the invaders in *The Andromeda Strain* (1971) are just viruses. Almost all the people in a small village are killed by the virus. A team of scientists tracks down the virus in a modern laboratory. The lab is set to destruct itself if the virus isn't destroyed within a certain time span. The end of the film is a race against the clock to switch off the bomb.

From giant reptiles to green men to slimy blobs, the movie invaders from outer space take many different forms. Here is a sample of some other movies that feature space monsters:

Beast with a Million Eyes (1955) has a mind-enslaving invader from outer space.

Brain from Planet Arous (1958) has another giant brain out to conquer Earth.

Daleks: Invasion Earth 2150 A.D. (1966) is a British film starring Peter Cushing, a well-known veteran of horror movies. This one is about an invasion of London by mechanical robots from space.

Earth vs. the Flying Saucers (1956) features a great battle in Washington, D.C., between the saucers and humans.

8·JOURNEY INTO SPACE

This Island Earth (1955) begins in familiar surroundings. But the story soon expands to include space travel and interplanetary war. The film shows a young scientist, played by Rex Reason, on a flight in his private jet. The plane develops engine trouble but is brought in for a safe landing by a strange green light.

Later, in his laboratory, other odd things begin to happen to Reason. He receives a mysterious electronics catalog. The catalog offers parts that are clearly not made on Earth. Working from plans and parts that are supplied to him seemingly from nowhere, Reason builds an "Interociter." A face appears on the screen of the Interociter and congratulates him on having passed his test. It tells him to expect a plane that will take him to his new job.

Reason becomes a member of a team of scientists

working on a plantation in Georgia. He discovers that his examiners are aliens. They have gathered together Earth's best scientific minds. They want help to find a way to save their planet, Metaluna, from destruction in an interplanetary war.

Matter transmitters beam the scientists through space to Metaluna. From a giant observation room in a flying saucer, they are shown the landscape of Me-

The clawed Mutant from *This Island Earth* (Universal).

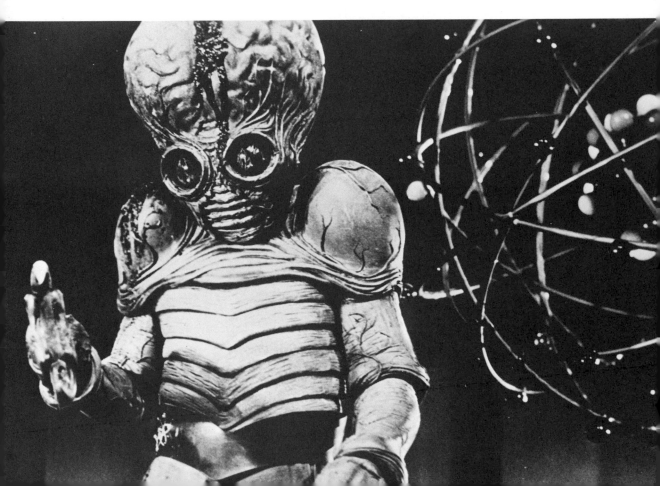

taluna. The neighboring planet Zahgon is hurling meteors down on the surface of Metaluna. The scene is dramatic, especially when viewed in the original wide-screen Cinemascope.

Among the excellent special effects in the movie are the big brains of the Metalunans and the even bigger brain of the clawed Mutant. The message of the film seems to be that Earth is just a little planet considered unimportant by the powerful worlds in the rest of the galaxy.

Another movie that has excellent special effects is *Forbidden Planet* (1956). A United Planets spaceship is on a mission to Altair IV. The crew is going to investigate what happened to a space colony planted on Altair IV years earlier. When they arrive, they find one survivor of the original colony. He is a language specialist, Morbius.

All the other colonists were killed by a planetary force. For some reason Morbius and his wife were immune, but his wife died later of natural causes. Their child, Alta, now a grown woman, lives with Morbius. Also with them is Robby the Robot, "master of 187 different languages." (For more about Robby, see page 30.)

The remains of a long-dead civilization lie buried beneath the planet. The builders of the civilization,

On the other side of the door is the evil monster of *Forbidden Planet* (MGM). Robby the Robot is the only one who doesn't look scared.

the Krell, also built Robby. And just as Robby is still in working order, the fantastic power below the surface is still available.

Soon the same force that killed the colonists is attacking the crew of the spaceship. The ship's doctor finds out that the "monster" is really the unconscious mind of Morbius, powered by the Krell's machinery.

In one of the final scenes, the evil monster is burning through a metal door twenty-eight inches thick. Morbius shouts, "My evil self is at the door, and I have no power to stop it."

Finally, Morbius throws himself at the door and dies. By dying, he throws a switch that will cause the planet to be destroyed in a few hours. Alta, Robby, and the remaining crew members watch from space as the planet explodes behind them.

In *It! The Terror from Beyond Space* (1958), the monster is a Martian reptile-type. It appears on board a human spaceship. After some bloody and destructive scenes the monster is shot through a hatchway into space.

Uranus is the destination for the spaceship in *Journey to the Seventh Planet* (1962). The crew of five Earthmen arrive on a planet that is ruled by a giant brain. The brain is able to make the Earthmen see any illusion it chooses. They meet a giant prehistoric monster (an illusion), some beautiful Earth girls (also whipped up by the brain in an illusion), and a barrier of energy. Breaking through the barrier, they freeze the brain with liquid oxygen. If your brain isn't frozen by the terrible acting, you might enjoy some of the special effects in the movie.

Voyage to a Prehistoric Planet (1965) is a Russian

Don't worry. Those teeth are just an illusion dreamed up by the giant brain in *Journey to the Seventh Planet* (American International).

movie that was first released under the title *Storm Planet.* A later production features some additional scenes in which the English-speaking actors Basil Rathbone and Faith Domergue appear. The story concerns the first landing on Venus.

The original Russian movie includes a cheerful robot and any number of alien life forms, some of which look like dinosaurs. The Venusian landscapes in the movie are very spectacular. The explorers on Venus travel around in a ship which can move on land, on water, and even underwater. The adventures are interesting but the dubbed English dialogue is very poor.

Much above the average science fiction movie is *Solaris* (1972), based on the novel by the Polish science fiction writer Stanislaw Lem. The setting is a station just above the surface of the mystery planet Solaris. The planet has been studied for many years by scientists. They are unable to agree as to its exact nature, but they know that the "ocean" which covers most of the planet seems to be a single living thing.

The station is now occupied by only three scientists. A "space psychologist" named Kelvin is sent from Earth. His job is to find out why the scientists' reports have become so peculiar. He arrives to find the station in a mess. One of the scientists is dead. The others refuse to discuss their experiences on the planet.

The next morning Kelvin awakes to find his wife beside him. The only problem is that his wife had killed herself on Earth ten years earlier. It turns out that each of the scientists has his own "visitor." It seems that the ocean is able to know the fears and memories of its human observers. It has made these memories into living models.

Kelvin begins to crack under the strain of events. But the other scientists figure out a way to send their conscious thoughts to the planet. The planet, which doesn't want to harm the observers, realizes its mistake and the "visitors" disappear. The film is beautifully photographed; especially good are the details of the space station.

But without a doubt the most beautifully photographed science fiction film ever made is *2001: A Space Odyssey* (1968). The story is by Arthur C. Clarke and the film was directed by Stanley Kubrick. The film really doesn't have a monster. But it does have strange black coffin-shaped slabs that give off

Astronauts find the slab on the Moon in *2001: A Space Odyssey* (MGM).

a piercing sound when uncovered. It also has a computer, HAL-9000, that goes mad and tries to destroy the occupants of a spaceship.

The film is in three parts. The first part takes place in primitive times when humans are little more than bands of apes. The second part takes place aboard a space shuttle and on a moon base. The final part takes place aboard a huge spaceship bound for Jupiter.

In the film, the large black slabs seem to be some kind of "alarm clocks" planted by a superior alien intelligence. The first slab is discovered on Earth by the primitive man-apes. The slab sends forth a sound which seems to teach the apes how to use a bone as a weapon.

On the way to Jupiter in *2001*.

The second slab is discovered in a crater on the moon. It sends off a sound which seems to be pointing at Jupiter. The third slab appears to the only astronaut left alive on the spaceship headed for Jupiter. Finally a fourth slab transforms the man into a "star baby" which floats off into space.

Just telling the story is not enough to make you really appreciate it. This is one film you must see. From the superbly photographed space station, to the rocket bound for Jupiter, to the weird images the astronaut sees, the film is a treat to your eyes, ears, and imagination.

9·SPACE MONSTERS ON TV

Who would ever think that a pointy-eared alien from the planet Vulcan would get thousands of fan letters from TV viewers? Of course the alien is Mr. Spock, first officer of the starship *Enterprise*. The TV program is "Star Trek," one of the most popular science fiction series ever shown.

"Star Trek" starred William Shatner as Captain James T. Kirk, Leonard Nimoy as Mr. Spock, and DeForest Kelley as Dr. Leonard McCoy. This show began in 1966 and never drew very large audience ratings. But every time the TV network decided to cancel the show, hundreds of thousands of fans wrote in to complain.

After three years, the show was canceled on network TV. But that was not the end of "Star Trek." Independent TV stations are still rerunning the episodes. At this writing, a New York TV station reruns

The alien Mr. Spock, first officer of the starship *Enterprise* in "Star Trek."

six "Star Trek" episodes every week! In addition, dozens of books about "Star Trek" have been published. Each year, a "Star Trek" convention draws thousands of fans called "trekkies."

A number of memorable space monsters appear in the stories. One of the most frightening is from a "Star Trek" show called "The Man Trap." This monster sucks all the salt out of people's bodies.

Two kinds of aliens that appeared in a number of episodes on "Star Trek" were the Romulans and the Klingons. The Romulans were an offshoot of the Vulcans. They all looked like Mr. Spock, with

The salt-eating monster from "The Man Trap" episode of "Star Trek."

pointed ears and arched eyebrows. The Klingons were bearded men with dark faces. They had bushy eyebrows that arched up at the ends. Both the Romulans and the Klingons were bad guys who opposed the good guys from the United Federation of Planets.

Perhaps the cutest, or at least the most appealing, of space "monsters" appeared in an episode called "The Trouble with Tribbles." Tribbles look like fluffy hamsters. They are adorable and affectionate. The trouble with them is that, like hamsters, they multiply and multiply—and multiply.

At about the same time that "Star Trek" was running on one network, another network was running a competing show called "Lost in Space." "Lost in

Space" featured a space explorer and his family, a funny but greedy and stupid doctor, and a handsome lieutenant. All were castaways on a distant planet. Most of the programs had one kind of space monster or another. "Lost in Space" seemed to be aimed at a much younger audience than "Star Trek" and never developed the same loyal following.

The most imaginative and frightening aliens from

One of the many monsters from "Lost in Space."

space appeared on a show called "The Outer Limits." It began in 1963 and ran for only two seasons. But almost every episode on the show had an excellent story and included a frightening monster.

The show used a different cast for each program. In the first episode, Cliff Robertson played a scientist who was trying to transport a being from the Andromeda Galaxy to Earth. In later episodes, Leonard Nimoy tried to clear a robot of murder charges, and William Shatner showed us how an astronaut just returned from Venus tried to stay warm. (Both were evidently warming up for their roles in "Star Trek.")

One of the best stories in the series was one in which Robert Culp played the character Trent in "Demon with a Glass Hand," by Harlan Ellison. Aliens are hunting Trent in a shadowy city. The aliens are from a future time. They wear medallions around their necks which keep them in this time. If a medallion is removed, the alien is shifted in agony into the future.

Trent's memory goes back only ten days. He is a grown man who does not know who he is, where he is, or why the aliens are after him. But Trent has a glass hand which tells him what to do. The hand tells him about the aliens' medallions. However, the hand

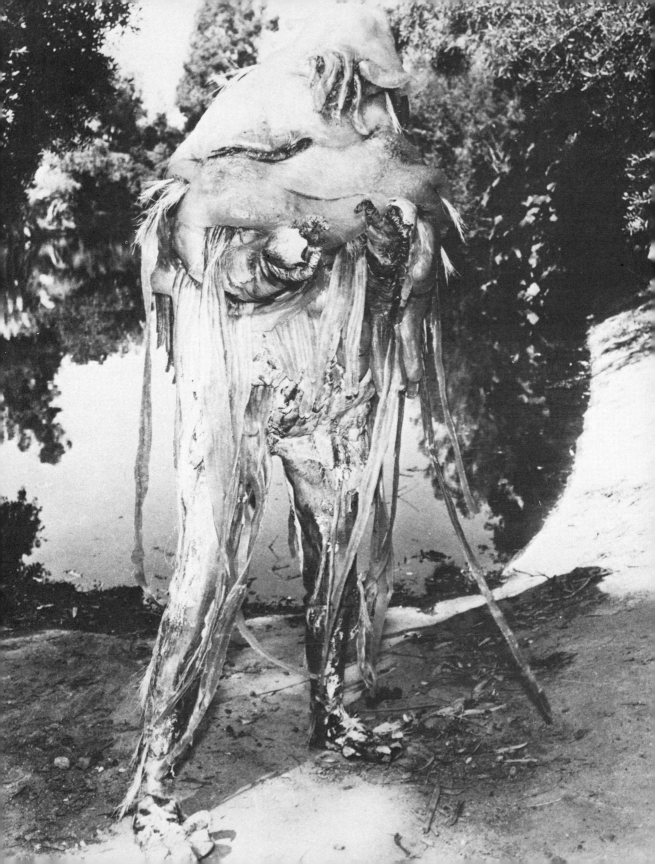

is lacking three fingers. Without them, the hand cannot tell Trent who he is or why he is in the city.

Trent hunts down the aliens and regains his missing fingers. It seems that Trent was sent back from the future to hide in the present. He is carrying all human knowledge and consciousness engraved on a single piece of wire. With the human race of the future beyond their reach, the aliens will leave. Humankind will wait until Trent has lived through the centuries to his own time. The long wait won't bother Trent. After all, his hand tells him, he's only a robot anyway.

In a two-part episode called "The Invisibles," George Macready plays an agent of an alien race that's out to conquer Earth. He lures men to a deserted army camp and straps them down to a bench. When they are helpless, he places insectlike aliens on their backs. The aliens penetrate the men's minds and take them over. The episode ends with a wounded man, played by Burt Reynolds, dragging himself through an empty factory while the aliens chase him.

Another TV series that was all about aliens was

A far-out monster from "The Outer Limits."

"The Invaders" (1967). In "The Invaders," Roy Thinness tried week after week to convince everybody that human look-alikes had started to take over Earth. Unfortunately, the aliens were not frightening. They looked just like humans except that they were unable to bend their little fingers.

A recent series about outer space is "Space: 1999." The story is written along the same lines as "Star Trek." The Moon blows out of orbit and is rocketed off into space. Each week there is an adventure as the satellite passes by a new planet or some object in space. The special effects on the program are very good, but the characters don't have the appeal of Captain Kirk and Mr. Spock.

Now that we've visited the Moon and sent space probes to Mars and Venus, is the day of the Bug-Eyed Monster over? Not at all. As long as we can use our imaginations, new and even more terrifying monsters will be on their way to Earth.

Another of the imaginative aliens that appeared in "The Outer Limits."

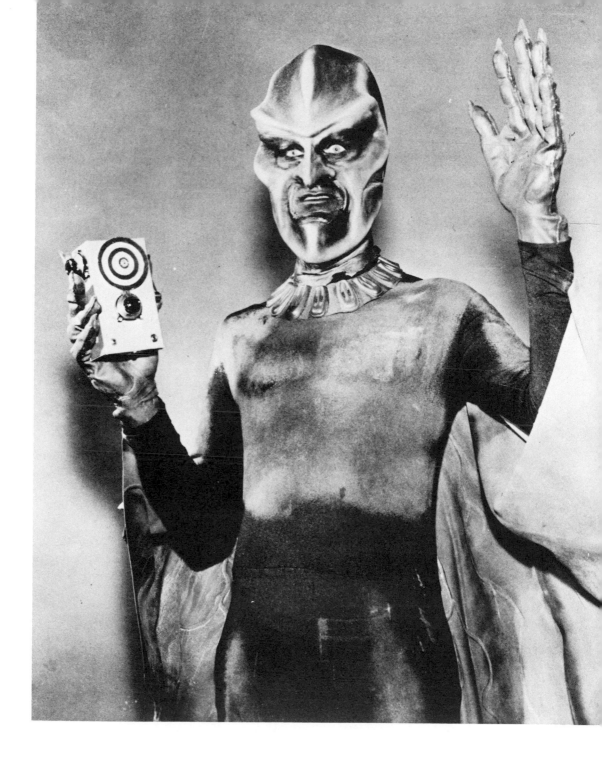

FILMS AND THEIR STUDIOS

The Andromeda Strain (1971) *Universal*

The Beast with a Million Eyes (1955) *American Releasing Corp.*

The Blob (1958) *Paramount*

Brain from Planet Arous (1958) *Howco International*

Buck Rogers (1939) *Universal*

The Colossus of New York (1958) *Paramount*

Commando Cody (1953) *Republic*

The Crawling Eye (1958) *DCA*

The Creeping Unknown (1955) *United Artists/Hammer* (The Quatermass Experiment)

Daleks: Invasion Earth 2150 A.D. (1966) *Amicus*

The Day of the Triffids (1962) *Allied Artists*

The Day the Earth Stood Still (1951) *Twentieth Century-Fox*

Earth vs. the Flying Saucers (1956) *Columbia*

Five Million Years to Earth (1968) *Twentieth Century-Fox/Hammer* (Quatermass in the Pit)

Flash Gordon (1936) *Universal*

Flash Gordon Conquers the Universe (1940) *Universal*

Flash Gordon's Trip to Mars (1938) *Universal*

Flying Disc Man from Mars (1951) *Republic*

Forbidden Planet (1956) *MGM*

Gog (1954) *United Artists*

I Married a Monster from Outer Space (1958) *Paramount*

Invaders from Mars (1953) *Twentieth Century-Fox*

Invasion of the Body Snatchers (1956) *Allied Artists*

Invasion of the Saucer Men (1957) *American International*

It Came from Outer Space (1953) *Universal*

It Conquered the World (1956) *American International*

It! The Terror from Beyond Space (1958) *United Artists*

Journey to the Seventh Planet (1962) *American International*

Kronos (1957) *Twentieth Century-Fox*

The Lost Planet (1953) *Republic*

The Man from Planet X (1951) *United Artists*

The Monolith Monsters (1957) *Universal*

The Mysterians (1958) *Toho*

The Mysterious Dr. Satan (1940) *Republic*

Mysterious Island (1951) *Columbia*

The Phantom Creeps (1939) *Universal*

The Phantom Empire (1935) *Mascot*

Radar Men from the Moon (1952) *Republic*

Solaris (1972) *Mosfilm*

Son of the Blob (1972) *Paramount*

Target Earth (1954) *Allied Artists*

The Thing from Another World (1951) *RKO*

This Island Earth (1955) *Universal*

Twenty Million Miles to Earth (1957) *Columbia*

2001: A Space Odyssey (1968) *MGM*

Undersea Kingdom (1936) *Republic*

Visit to a Small Planet (1960) *Paramount*

Voyage to a Prehistoric Planet (1965) *New Realm* (Storm Planet)

War of the Worlds (1953) *Paramount*

INDEX